The Civil War

The Civil War

It Ain't Over Yet!

Lance Carden

Foreword by Griffith H. Williams

RESOURCE *Publications* · Eugene, Oregon

THE CIVIL WAR
It Ain't Over Yet!

Resource Publications
An Imprint of Wipf and Stock Publishers
199 W. 8th Ave., Suite 3
Eugene, OR 97401

www.wipfandstock.com

PAPERBACK ISBN: 978-1-6667-1264-3
HARDCOVER ISBN: 978-1-6667-1265-0
EBOOK ISBN: 978-1-6667-1266-7

AUGUST 9, 2021

To all our descendants

Contents

EARTH HISTORY

PERSONAL HISTORY

Foreword

THIS VOLUME REVEALS THE multiple layers of poet Lance Carden. New readers will be fascinated by the wide range of his work. For those who have followed his words over the years, this collection contains many of the elements we have come to look forward to in his writing. Here are deep metaphors. There is clever wordplay. Everywhere is a profound sense of honesty.

Within this volume you will find history, spirituality, and an environmental outlook. Family, relationships, and geographic wanderings all have a part to play in these poems. Sports and the great game of politics are represented. Gentle humor and respect for the reader are everywhere. In other words, this book illuminates an authentic poet.

The poems are grouped into three chapters. The first, "Our Civic History," deals with racial equity, social justice, history, and politics. From Carden's first book *Witness: An Oral History of Black Politics in Boston* (1989) to his newest play, *Democracy's Demise* (2018), these topics have consistently drawn his attention.

Geography is central to Carden's ability to deal with issues surrounding race and politics. Raised in Oklahoma, he comes from the heartland, but he has lived most of his adult life in the costal corners of the country. He has called the north home, and the south, the east, and the west. That broad perspective informs his poetry. An Air Force veteran, Carden is an optimistic patriot whose vision for the nation focuses on a never-ending journey toward improvement.

The second chapter is "Earth History." Here are poems exploring our relationship to the environment. From the microcosm of a zoo's butterfly house to the global patterns of hurricanes, Carden looks at humanity's role in balancing the great equation of life. As always, he uses carefully constructed verse, rich in rhythm and rhyme, to convey his message. Readers of his earlier volume, *Spiritual Exercise* (2019), will find a direct line between that poetry book and this. His internal sense of timing, urgent as an orchardman preparing to prune, reminds us that everything has a proper season. In terms of attending to the Earth's changing environment, that time may indeed be now!

The third chapter, "Personal History," is a delightful mosaic of places and people. It would seem as if most journeys in his life have provided Carden with insights or observations worthy of a poem. He first explored these themes in *Tuscan Retreat* (2013), a book of poetry about Italy co-written with his wife, Charlene Vincent. The present volume takes us from Mount Rainier to Habana, Cuba, and beyond.

At other times, he follows a path he first walked as a poet in *City of Lions* (2015), digging into the heart and soul of whatever place presently happens to be home. When Carden digs deep, the people he uncovers are always memorable. In this volume, he mainly portrays family, from siblings to cousins, even an old orange tabby cat named Marmalade. Each is captured clearly, as in a snapshot. Even if you never knew any of these people, you feel some recognition, for Carden shines a light on their shared humanity.

We also find some insight into the creation of these rather serious poems. Carden includes a lovely shape poem discussing his writing process. And several poems later, he explores the mystery of mystery for all poets: Where do our poems come from? In one titled "Our Poems Take Their Own Time," Carden reports that the best of them: " . . . unfold / like some refined / lotus flower, / floating in a fertile mind."

With that, gentle reader, please leave this introduction and turn your attention to these vivid poems, blooming with wit and wisdom.

Griffith H. Williams is a Seattle-based poet who has illustrated and printed dozens of chapbooks on his own antique Chandler & Price letterpress.

OUR CIVIL HISTORY

Our Civil War

It was not a war North nor South
  would ever
   have fought,
had they known marching in
   the untold cost
   of staggering out.

Total victory left the North
   wounded
   but self-righteous,
while most Southerners felt
   the horror & self-pity
   of defeat.

Few people would summarize
   our bloody brawl
by saying the survivors
   were now "indivisible
   with liberty
   & justice for all."

But at least our young country,
   big & strong,
   now aligned
with the more hopeful side
   of history
   & morality.

You're either for human rights
& reparations,
or you're for more racial strife
& aggravations.

Bedlam in Babel

Americans in red & blue
        have split
our English tongue
        in two:
Two political cultures,
        misuse
two distinct lingos,
        to feed feuds
between two broods
        afraid to lose.

Red won't hear what
        Blue's got to say,
or even care what Blue
        wants to do.
Blue's all fed up
        with all things Red;
& could care less
        what things he's said.

Wars are always uncivil
        in a nation state,
but in these so-called
        United States,
the babbling & bedlam
        of Babel
have become our common—
        yes, appalling—fate.

Fort Sumter, Charleston

What the casual tourist
        continues to visit,
        a wartime relic,
is perhaps poor reward
        for the long, long
        ferry queues, but
        views of the harbor
can seem quite sweet,
        & the breezes offer
        some relief
from the steam of summer
        & the oppressive heat.

This is where they lit the fuse
        for the entire
        Civil War,
& few targets were more burned
        by canon fire
than this pivotal point
        of no return.

The worn-down federal fort
        still seems defiant
& capable of evoking
        or contaminating
a vast sea of volatile emotions,
        long distilled,
but largely undigested,
        seven-score years
        & more

since our shotgun matrimony
        of misfits
        was determined
by the outcome of the war:

Two ever-quarrelling parties,
        blue & gray—
the gray now turned blood-red—
        trying to sail
        one ship
        with conflicting charts
& a very long voyage ahead.

The Civil War may be bygone
        for those of us
        up in Beantown,
but, for folks way-way down
        in Dixie,
        it ain't over yet!

---

* *First written April 12, 2011, on the 150th anniversary of the South Carolina Militia attack on Union forces at Fort Sumter in Charleston Harbor, triggering the Civil War*

THE SHAW MEMORIAL

There goes the Massachusetts 54th,
        their eyes upon the prize;
that most would die in sacrifice
        should come as no surprise.

What makes the black troops so willing?
        Might they be insane?
With better ways to be employed,
        would they have done the same?

The officer in the foreground,
        below the charming angel,
sits rigid in the saddle
        & far above the sod.

He's a white youth from Harvard
        with the golden name of Shaw;
they all have a date with glory,
        but his fame alone will glow.

That angel soaring way up high,
        why is she so resigned?
Have these men been mesmerized?
        Do we see this in their eyes?

That busy little drummer
        seems to unify the throng.
Can you sense his rat-a-tat hammer,
        forcing them along?

Or is it perhaps invisible,
      something that cannot sing?
Centuries of persecution
      can leave a psychic sting.[*]

[*] *The Robert Gould Shaw Memorial is a large bas-relief by Augustus Saint-Gaudens across the street from the Massachusetts State House in Boston Common.*

Bay State Blues

Outside my Beantown window,
    I spot a flock
    of blackbirds
    as they glide
through swirling sheets
    of sleet & snow,
outfighting a nor'easter
    with power
    of flight.

Then I compare how dire
    350 years ago,
    the plight
    in the Bay Colony
of that small original band
    of African slaves
    who were mired
    down below
with barrels of salt & tobacco
    on a Salem ship
    their owners
    called *Desire*.

Freighted north from tropical
    Caribbean sand—
then stranded, shackled
    in this wintered land.[*]

* *Written in February 1988, the 350th anniversary of the arrival in the Massachusetts Bay Colony of the first group of black slaves to reach the colony in February 1638*

CRISPUS ATTUCKS

In sunny Boston Common,
        no clouds or crowds about,
I'm seeking Crispus Attucks
        & sorting history out.

Below the State House door,
        on Gaudens' bas-relief,
I watch as Regiment 54
        marches off to civil gore.

Then I discover Attucks
        down by Tremont Street,
struck by British muskets
        & blown clear off his feet.

Though he's not able to answer me,
        I'd like to pose two questions
to this fallen Doodle Dandy,
        our first in history:

Did you, my dark-skinned rowdy,
        think yourself a Yankee?
Or did you believe our Revolution
        would set the black man free?[*]

---

  * *Crispus Attucks was a runaway slave who was apparently first to fall in the 1770 Boston Massacre, as depicted graphically on a memorial in Boston Common. Augustus Saint-Gaudens' monument to the 54th Regiment is also in the Common.*

LIBERATING THE SLAVES

In a very large monument
          to emancipation,
in downtown Boston,
          dated 1879,
President Abraham Lincoln
          is allegedly shown
          unchaining
all our American slaves.

At my accidental visit, a few
          twigs, a stone,
          & a feather
had been fitted together
          before the sculpture,
          as though
          something holy
were somehow buried there.

"A race set free & the country
          at peace,"
an inscription testified,
          penned long after
          Lincoln was shot dead
& blacks down South deprived
          of whatever rights
might otherwise have survived.*

---

* *This sculpture, which was located next to the Park Plaza Hotel, is a copy of one Thomas Ball designed for Lincoln Park in Washington, D.C. The controversial Boston monument was removed by the Boston Art Commission in December 2020, long after the writing of this poem.*

RECONSTRUCTION

We were, in retrospect,
     quite wacky
     to restrict
     Reconstruction
     to old Dixie
& those post-Civil War years.

The real reconstruction,
     sorely needed,
     is a perpetual
     all-citizen
     determination
to live up to the Constitution.

In this mental redirection,
     there is
     certainly
     work for
     everyone—
& much reflection to be done.

Quantum Politics

I freely admit I don't understand
        quantum physics,
but "quantum politics"—
            well, since I just
            made this up,
            I suppose
some explanation is a must:

It's when people are so divided
           that even the most
obvious fact, figure,
           or phenomenon
seems dependent on the observer.

For instance: What is a protest
           or a riot?
What is cancel culture
           or climate change?
What's a lie, a racist, or a bigot?

In general, we have trouble
           with these ideas
because people perceive them
           with different eyes
& all are so mesmerized
           by hate or ill will
that tossing bias in the dump
           takes a quantum jump.

Our Once-Grand Flag

Recently, I was brought full stop
       by a wooden flag
in the window of a barber shop
       in St. Augustine.

As this piece of art came into vision,
       I sat in the barber's chair
beneath the red-&-white stripes
       of yet another version
of our nation's glorious banner.

When I beheld the statuette,
       maybe only
       two-by-four feet,
I realized the blue, white, & red
       were held together
by a little beam of naked
       barbed wire,
       which also snaked
around the artwork's frame.

This image made me wonder:
       Who should we upbraid
that affections which used to glue
       red & blue together
are now barbed with hate,
       each of the other?

St. Augustine

We wander here & revel
        among some truly
        grand old ruins,
        a few still above,
        but now mostly
well below ground level.

Even remnants still in view
        have lost most
        of what context
        might best
        reveal to us
their true historical value.

We simply cannot behold
        the old market
        as slave families,
        locked in chains,
        were marched here
to be either bought or sold.

For me, the discussion
        of which relics
        of the Civil War
        to retain or ponder
        raises another,
even more aching question:

How can this old beloved
          conquistador hub,
          born in blood,
          be freshly bathed
          or somehow reborn
in compassion & love?

Why White Ain't So Neat

I have been wondering
        how I might
        best suggest
        a new category
        of human being,
one we might call "off white"?

Some absolute display
        of whiteness,
or total absence of color,
        seems appropriate
for more formal attire or
        for the sheets
        of the KKK,
but could we not eliminate
        the term "white"
        from discourse
about race or peoples,
        who are almost
        never really so—
excepting, of course—
        those born albinos.

A Strange Fruitage

When I see old Southern oaks
      & other trees
      with ragged strands
      of grayish "hair,"
I don't think of this growth
      as Spanish moss
      or some kind of floss;
      instead, I bear witness
to the remains of thousands
      of black bodies,
      faded & wasted,
      still hanging up there—
& swinging softly to or fro,
      if & whenever
      re-troubled
      by some whip of air.

OUR FRACTIOUS DEMOCRACY

This is a democracy, a country
      where people supposedly free
      can fight for liberty,
& this has been our history:
      relatively "good" people
      opposed by "evil" people,
who don't want them to be free.

Some of the "evil," mostly "white" men,
      are now rocking the boat,
because they feel they've been
      losing out since women,
blacks, & others won the right to vote.

Perhaps these men are reversing
      a positive trend,
      though exactly
how much no one yet can tell.

The two sides will probably
      go on warring,
      tooth & nail,
at least at the ballot box, until
      there are no more people
or a whole lot less of evil.

Backlashed?

Of course, we can't hold Africa
    responsible
    for all those
block-buster super-hurricanes
    drifting west
    from the sub-Sahara
to our most Southern shores.

There is, however, I suspect,
    some sort
    of reckoning
    in the fact
that these storms begin as tiny
    disturbances off
    the African coast
& then, collecting energy
    from warm waters
    as they grow,
retrace the many voyages
    of slave ships
transporting human cargo
    to our ports
not all that many years ago.

These eruptions wreak havoc
    in the same areas
    of our country
which once arrogated
    to themselves
    millions
    of African slaves

who were denied any rights
        as people
& where the scientific claim
        of human-aided
        climate change
is so vociferously negated.

This leads at least me to think
        there may be
        some serial link
        of denial
connecting the old South's
        slave wounds
to these new disasters,
        now so seemingly
        perennial.

DONALD VS. HILLARY

This is not just a choice of
        him or her,
        conserve or lib,
        elephant or mule;
we're forced to decide whether
        the crude or the civil,
        a canon or a baton,
        a divider or a uniter,
        a passion or a vision,
        a ruler or a servant
will march us back into the past
        or forward
        to the future—
in so, so many ways
        just another phase
of our same old, same old
        Civil War.

BLACK LIVES MATTER

I grew up in Oklahoma, thinking
       there was something
       obviously wrong
in the so-called "black" community—
       not just poverty,
but something more hostile
       & unsightly,
a decadence that as a teenager
       I could not define.

Why should we, I would muse,
       want to dance & sing
       to some new
       rock-&-roll song
the same way *those* people do?

Now, as I'm increasingly aware
       & in awe
of the spirit & creativity
       of African-Americans,
I feel the bitter irony
       of them having to
       point out to me
the selfish bigotry & apathy
       of so-called
       "white" society.

A Bad Joke

I like a really good joke,
       & who doesn't?

A good joke will unite
       people;
a bad one divide them,
       should they
       condone it.

A *really* bad joke is when
       someone
       feels so much pain
that it's not even
       polite
       to retell it,
or laugh out loud,
       or grin.

Some might call this
       "politically
       correct,"
but, mostly, it's just
       etiquette.

Putin Pulls the Strings

Viewed in its full precision,
    the amazing stunt
Vladimir Putin was able
    to arrange
during our strange
    2016 election
    was an act
some militarists would call
    "regime change."

The Russian President
    not only
    successfully fought
to shove a special friend
    or accomplice
into the Oval Office,
    but did this
    from without
like a master puppeteer
    without forfeit
    of even a soldier
or the firing a single shot.

ME FOR PRESIDENT?

When I was a young boy,
      it was said
anyone could be President,
      even *me*,
though I could never quite
      believe it,
assuming it would have to be
      somebody
obviously, undeniably
      right.

But now, with Donald J. Trump
      as President,
my future term as POTUS
      seems more probable
with just a bit of impetus
      & a great big jump.*

---

* *I'm Lance Carden, and I approve this commercial.*

27

Survival

The dire question raised
    by the election
    of Donald Trump
    is not whether
the new President
    can or cannot
    withstand
the violent political storm
    he has
    purposely
    created,
but if our delicate form
    of democracy
    also can.

As Virus Numbers Start Rising Again

In the Battle of the Virus,
        or Covid vs. Fauci,
President Trump's deciding
        with obvious dread:
"Dr. Fauci is losing,
        a worrisome trend;
so, I'm joining with Covid,
        Mr. Covid, instead.
Dr. Fauci is losing—
        so, off with his head!

"Let's everyone get sick
        & then jump into bed;
it's better for business,
        & I'll win in the end.
So, I'm joining with Covid
        to immune the whole herd;
all the others are suckers,
        or losers, instead.
Dr. Fauci is losing—
        so, off with his head!"

The Trump Obsession

Our dear, dear President,
       Donald Trump,
is so overly intoxicated
       with himself,
his many tweets, reality TV,
       & his personality
that finally, at the end
       of his term,
he can't accept the possibility,
       the "irreality,"
of defeat, or stepping down;
       & many others
in the GOP are wont to consume
       a similar potion
for they have now begun
       to nurture
his obsession: our first *Führer*
       to become.

When the 'News' Gets You Down

Yes, there may be more
         fake news
& abuse in the air
         today than before—
more error to ensnare
         & drive to despair
those unadvised
         that the greater
         the errors
& the size of the lies
         the more sure
         is the future
of their *total* demise.

To the Far Right

You seem to have built
        together
        for yourselves
a great big bunker of hate
        that's so far
        invulnerable
to the gifting of feathers,
        flowers, or
        similar treasure,
so, I'm breeding a healthier,
        stealthier
        sort of dove,
which, unlike traditional
        coal-mine canaries,
        will be immune
to all venoms & the refusals
        thus far to you of
        my brotherly love.

Divided We Fall

The history of humanity's
     violent vendettas—
so cruel, harrowing, & full
     of confusion—
seems to confirm a caution
     that rings down
     through the ages,
even from Confucius,
     one of China's
     foremost sages:
"Before you embark on
     a journey of revenge,
     dig two graves."*

---

* *This poem first appeared in a book titled* Tuscan Retreat *in* 2013.

EARTH HISTORY

Our Mother Earth

We're all the children of God,
          just happy to be alive;
we know we have a higher life,
          but here we hug the Earth.

She lends us what we wear,
          gives also what we eat.
Could we live without her?
          Oh, that we could not bear!

Her eyes are ever open;
          she knows where she goes.
She keeps on moving forward;
          we're glad for what she knows.

She knows that we are foolish
          & prone to make mistakes;
she takes it with a steady smile
          & never us forsakes.

We're sorry if we've abused her,
          or caused her any pain;
she's such a super Mother,
          let's not do that again!

Even if you never despoil her,
          as most people do;
you must work with us together
          to see our Mother through.

We think she's growing thinner,
   as we grow in number.
Let's promise to be kinder
   & take good care of her.

For the Earth needs us, also,
   to ration some of her parts.
Yes, folks have selfish egos,
   but *all* love her in our hearts.

Sooner the Better

That giant limb sawed off the pine
       has left behind an oval scar;
concentric circles, twenty-nine,
       leak amber tears soft as tar.

A victim of nothing but neglect,
       the tree was surely going to fall;
some owners it could not select
       in pruning took no stock at all.

How blessed this pine tree might have been,
       had the seedling known how to grow;
it would have seemed gentle way back then,
       a little grooming years ago.

So, what's to take from all of this,
       & what should each of us know?
Just as nature knows to nurture us,
       in her, we play a major role.

History Recycled?

If human events were
       repeating
       themselves,
       like so many
       reruns
       of old movies,
then every time around,
       wouldn't
       even the most
       spine-chilling
       of contingencies—
       even a pandemic—
seem ever-less confounding?

But this is far from true:
       For most of us,
       each & every crisis—
       be it some drought
       or a virus uprising—
       seems somehow new
& often quite surprising.

Any universal index
       of nasty black holes
       would surely show
       that those most abject
       exist, not someplace
       in outer space,
but in some history text.

HOUSTON REPEATS DUNKIRK MIRACLE

Is it merely a historical quirk
      that the movie *Dunkirk*
is playing in theaters this week
      even as hundreds
of private boats in Houston
      are picking up
      from flood waters
      of Hurricane Harvey
some hundreds of survivors
      who might otherwise
      have drowned,
      much the same way
many thousands of Allied soldiers
      found transport
across the English Channel
      from Dunkirk, France,
more than seventy years ago
      to a friendlier,
      safer shore?

And let's not forget to declare,
      beyond the coincidence,
that both historic events share
      a certain magnificence!*

---

* *In 1940, more than three hundred thousand British, French, and Belgian troops were evacuated by sea—many in private boats—from the port of Dunkirk to Great Britain and thus saved from being killed or captured by more powerful German forces. Hurricane Harvey hit Texas in 2017.*

Climate Change

Do you recall the great debate
        before World War II
which left our country late—
        just one step away
        from checkmate?

Well, it seems to me
        that climate change
is likely to be hopelessly
        subject to debate
until it's too hopelessly,
        hopelessly late
for people to adjust
        to our common fate.

The world, in my opinion,
        is facing
        a dilemma:
either sharing our resources
        & saving the environs,
or just squaring off
        against one another
        & bombing
the whole Earth to oblivion.

Be Cool!

We will not even begin
      to subdue
      the threat
of global warming
      until
      throughout
      the world
a whole lot more people
      learn how
      to abate
the escalating flame
      of human hate,
& then hopefully we'll
      all recall
      or reclaim
our lost ability to chill.

Urban Python

Every once in a while
        in St. Augustine,
        the peace
of our estuary is broken
        by some motorbike
        or hotrod
        over on Highway 1,
or by the alarming siren
        of an emergency vehicle,
        or by the din
        of a helicopter,
reminding us we're in
        an urban sprawl
        that began
        centuries ago
with invaders from Spain
        & is now
        devouring
our remaining terrain
        like a python
        in a pig pen.

Butterfly Zoo

I think there's something wrong
     with an artist
     who kills birds
in order to paint them,
     something wrong
     with a writer-scientist
who kills butterflies
     to study them,
& something wrong
     with a museum
     that exhibits
non-native butterflies,
     but will not
permit them to propagate,
     for whatever reason.

It's abhorrent to abuse
     or to manipulate
     any species
     for research,
for exhibit, or even for art—
     & especially
     for financial gain,
even to a so-called not-for-profit.

It's way too late for J. J. Audubon
     or for Vladimir Nabokov,
but not yet too late for reform
     at the University
     of Florida

& some similar museums
which permit
a form of slavery
in a beautiful, but artificial,
butterfly exhibit.

BUILT BY DEMONS

In a dream, I saw a couple
   of demons
   working like
   the very devil
to build something I couldn't
   quite make out;
   so, I decided
   to shout:

"What are you doing out there?"

"We're building walls."

"At the Mexican border?"

"No, we're separating rich
   from poor, North
   from South, whites
   from blacks."

"What's the barrier?"

"A simple composite
   of lies & fear."

"Any other walls?"

*"One designed to separate
almost everyone
from other people,
though not from us."*

"What's it called?"

"The coronavirus."

The Virus Room

Boom, boom—the virus room:
    Everything's
    suddenly
    out of focus;
    no one's ready
for this very naughty virus.

Zoom, zoom—the virus room:
    No one's coming,
    no one's going,
    few out eating,
    most retreating.

Kaboom, kaboom—the virus room:
    No one dating,
    no one necking,
    few out dancing,
    no one chancing;
some no longer even sensing.

Lives are staggering out of tune:
    Viruses here,
    viruses there;
    suddenly
    up-sucking
all of the air in the room!

Yes, dread Virus, in every Zoom,
    every conference,
    or invention,
    you loom
    the sickliest yet,
even in human imagination!

Extreme Radicals

When those extreme radicals,
  summer & winter,
struggle for climate control—
  one seemingly
  mild mannered
  & kind,
  the other brutal
  & intensely cold—
force yourself to remember,
  especially
  in July
  or late December,
the way you've beheld
  so many
  other years
  unfold:

You may have endured
  madcap winters,
& torrid, tropical summers,
  but neither ever
  beats the other:
By March or September,
  their bleak fits
of extreme distemper
  soon blow over,

& then a predictable
    change of season
    will pull one
    or the other,
back into another deep
    & hopefully
    peaceful sleep.

To a Bust of Pericles

Oh, blind & silent Pericles,
        do you somehow foresee
the end of humanity, maybe
        in a chat with Socrates?

Now, as the long fearful story
        oh-so-slowly unfolds,
can you preview the finale
        of the long, long scroll?

If so, through that full beard
        & small mouth obscure,
please at least whisper
        what we most need to hear,

sharing perhaps some wisdom
        from the bitter past,
revealing some sort of vision
        we've not so far grasped.

PERSONAL HISTORY

Personal History

There will be no piece
    of history
    or herstory
    for you or me;
we're way too ordinary,
    insufficiently
    ornery
    or honorary,
for pages or even traces
    in the ranks
    of daring doers
    destined
to be at least footnoted
    in the afterglow
    of what
    will then
be called "the long, long ago."

MY SCRIBBLING*

To the
 literary critic,
  my scribblings
   will contribute
    to "real poetry"
    the same way
   that jazz may
  add to what
 some
  call
   "classical music."

My idea being
        to make it
        a little
        more
        fun
         !

* *Reader beware: As an e-book, this shape poem may lose its intended shape.*

My Poet Cousin

My poet cousin,
       David Burch,
seldom ventured
       into church,
nor published much
       his pleasant verse.

So, it hit him
       with a certain
       puzzling surprise
to wake up
       in heaven
with a Pulitzer Prize!

Trump & My Brother

David, my younger brother,
        now deceased, would
otherwise try to muster
            whatever smut
            he could find
on President Donald J. Trump.

David kept a mental dossier
            on every prominent
            Republican
& knew exactly what to fear
            from whom,
& who might be sincere.

He grew up in Oklahoma,
            vulnerable
            & sensible,
because he was gay,
            & he died,
embittered but wise,
            from complications
            of AIDS.

He watched many a soul mate
            succumb to
            the same malady,
even as they were blamed
            morally
            for their fate

by pretentious politicians.
        So, for David,
        such affairs of state
were taken very personally.

To know that Donald Trump
        is a protégé
        of Roy Cohn,
who whispered in McCarthy's ear
        & helped dispatch
        the Rosenbergs,
would have fixed Trump
        in my brother's mind
        as evil incarnate—
or something like Frankenstein
        resurrected
        in pinstripes.

I do not hate the Donald;
        I feel somewhat
        sorry for him.
But I know my brother *would*.

The Other Marathon

Their bomb has dug a crater
        in my heart,
        which I am filling
        with my love—
not solely for the dears
        who died,
but, too, for the poor killers
        who, deceiving
        themselves,
conceived of this deep dark pit,
        & now must fill it
        with their tears,
which, mixing chemically
        with my love,
will slowly re-establish
        in my heart of hearts
a lost sun-filled meadow
        & its turtle dove.*

---

* *Written after the Boston Marathon bombing in 2013*

Lamb of Phlox

I came across a lamb of phlox
      lying on the ground,
      knee high,
its pinkish-purple blossoms bright,
      resplendent
      in meridian light.

I gave it lots of water
      & left it tethered there
to expand & bloom
      some other year,
perhaps as two full-grown sheep,
      waist deep,
frolicking in the summer breeze,
      the firstlings of a flock.

Our Poems Take Their Own Time

Like any love affair,
        our poems evolve
from fairly rare,
        but quite fanciful
leaps of human faith.

A poem, both wise & bold,
        doesn't ever
        grow solely
in ink or on lined paper,
        but will rather
        quickly or slowly
in one's own soul unfold
        like some refined
        lotus flower,
floating in a fertile mind.

So, my joy overflows
        if & when,
a slumbering poem begins
        to blossom
like a late-summer rose.

Double Entendre

When you start taking
      seemingly
      ordinary words
& tweaking them
      successfully
      into metaphors,
they are suddenly
      multitasking,
      & so are you—
desperately casting about
      in the ocean
      of language
for a fishy miracle phrase
      that can fill
      some verbal void
with golden coins in the gill.

Something, Something

When I heard the birds
        scatter,
I knew it was certain
        to rain.

No entrails were needed
        to explain,
there was nothing
        from the brain.

Something, one might say
        was in hiding,
had stepped into day
        from night,

but when I went to shut
        the windows,
something didn't seem
        quite right.

PEACOCKS IN HAVANA

They were much the same
         as we experienced
         elsewhere in Havana—
a muster of flamboyant birds,
         strutting a gaudy shape
         & stunning colors
         up & down
the manicured grounds
         of the Hotel Nacional,
         parading
for the whole world
         to see
their jaunty dominion
         & native pride.

But, oh! what an inward heartache
         was unloosed
when one of those cheeky peacocks
         would begin
         to croon
one of their interminable,
         unbearably
         gruesome
         bird songs—
a sudden, uneasy tutorial
         in Cuba's
         internal blues.

In Motion

I thought I could see
   a peach color
   in the breast
of a mourning dove
   as it strode
   peacefully
down my gabled roof
   & hopped
   ever so gently
into a myrtle tree
   outside
   a window,
where I was trying
   to write
   "poetry."

Nest Egg

In a giant crepe myrtle
      outside
      our front door,
two fat mourning doves,
      singing & cooing,
      coming & going,
are building a castle
      like two
      crackerjack
      entrepreneurs,
building their futures
      stick by stick,
eagerly anticipating
      a powerful
      nest egg—
interest compounding
      hour by hour.

RETIREMENT

Can you recall the marvel
           most people feel
the first time they're able
           to ride a bicycle?

Did someone run along
           beside you
as you clung to the handles
           & pumped
           on the pedals?

Was there a moment when
           that someone
decided to let you go,
           & of a sudden
you were on your own,
           but didn't
           really know?

Well, retirement is very close
           to that,
           but with vertigo.

It's like you're biking along
           some river
at a very dusky hour
           of day,
with no thoughts whatsoever
           about

what may be guiding you
         that way,
until you hear someone shout
         "Time out!"

Suddenly, the river stops running,
         & there's
         a humming
         in the air;
your feet go on peddling,
         but the ground's
         no longer there;

your wheels are still spinning,
         but you're in some
         new dimension—
up amid the moon & stars
         in some sort
         of suspended
         animation,
a thing you're now learning
         for a yet higher
         occupation.

Oklahoma Evening Song

My rounded mouth
      opens to inquire,

but creates a tremor
      in the air

like the low whistle
      of a Coke bottle:

solo flute accidental
      with cricket choir.

Hot Air Balloons

At long last, proverbially,
    the "hot" air
    has come out
    of the balloon
which Charlene & I
    purchased
    for my sister
    more than
    a month ago,
on her seventy-first.

It now declaims,
    "Happy Birthday!"
    to the floor,
as though no longer proud
    of its rather
    childish
    cliché.

For this aging family,
    energy seems
    to seep
    steadily
    these days,
from lots of "balloons"
    in many
    different ways,
though, as the stock market
    is wont
    to say,
"actual rates may vary."

FROG LEGS

Our three-day sibling reunion
        was framed
        in frog legs,
a joke so poor I had to force
        myself
        to laugh,
not wanting to embarrass
        an older brother
        we call Skooter,
who seemed to find it
        terribly
        funny
for a male customer
        to ask
        his waitress:
"Do you have frog legs?"
        & then—
if the answer were "Yes"—
        to suggest
she needs some medical test.

But, as is not unusual
        for Skooter,
        an octogenarian,
he kept on periodically
        referring
        to frog legs;
        for instance, asking
my sister, Lexa, if she had
        frog legs,
        and then asking me

if I were perhaps attracted
          to frog legs
          until we
          were both
laughing along with him,
          in hysterics,
not just at his corny joke,
          but also,
          in part,
          because
          as kids,
years ago in Oklahoma,
          we had often
          hunted
          for bullfrogs
with flashlights & frog gigs,
          & then watched
          their legs
          jump about
          in the frypan
when Mom cooked them up—
          & we laughed,
          too, in part,
because we remembered,
          even as a kid,
he could get & keep us
          laughing
          hour after hour,
sometimes day after day,
          hoping
          he'd desist
& really trying to resist
          his silly
          egocentric way

of making
everyone in earshot
defer to his
obvious
quite infectious
sort of humor
& his ability to make us roar
again & again,
many times over.

There's No Place Like a Caboose

From early childhood,
        my mother never
        loved anything
        like a train,
        & in a "choo-choo"
found nothing so amusing
        as the little caboose.

Velma & her whole family
        often took
        long vacations
        by train
for they could ride for free
        to places like Boston
        or Washington, D.C.,
but my mom also liked
        to go along
        with her daddy
on an occasional jaunt
        to train
        some young puppy
        how to hunt.

They'd climb aboard a caboose
        at the little station
        in Sapulpa,
        where Nat Burch,
        my grandpa,
was a teletype operator
        on the Santa Fe line,

& then they would enjoy the ride
                across the countryside
                to an isolated vale
                or forest,
where the train would brake
                so they could step off,
& Nat could shoot some rabbits,
                or pheasants,
                or quail.

And then, hours later, they would
                wave down
                another locomotive,
heading the opposite way,
                to take them,
                the hound,
                & any quarry
back to their little boom town.

Once all were back on board,
                Velma might slip
                into some bedding
                on the caboose,
because, even in Oklahoma,
                you can often
                see your breath
                produce a mist
as a slowly rising sun
                reveals the tracks
                behind a choo-choo
& a seemingly frozen horizon.

My dear mother was brought up
        to conceive of life
        as nearly divine,
& she stuck with that design
        till she was
        eighty-nine.

Time Runs Out

My grandfather's pocket timer,
      24-karat,
      hangs by a nail
      next to the door
where I hung it after
      an expensive repair
forced by my dropping it
      on the floor.

I thought, if I hung it there,
      I'd surely remember
      to wind it at least
      once each twenty-four,
      but I can now say
I was rather optimistic
      that I would actually
      notice it that way.

"Presented to N. H. Burch
      Grand Division,
Order of Railroad Telegraphers
      June 9th, 1911,
for meritorious service"
      is engraved
      on an inside panel
      of the back
of this ponderous tick tock.

So, today it's still hanging there
        by the door,
        stuck at 6:24,
        a stark reminder
        that in his grave
out in Oklahoma somewhere
        my dear grandfather,
unlike his frozen, golden timer,
        is probably
        rolling
        over & over.*

* Nathan Burch is also the grandfather of David Burch, mentioned in "My Poet Cousin" earlier in this volume. Nat's widow, Elizabeth Burch, lived with me and my family the whole time I was growing up. My full name is Lance Burch Carden.

Olympic Sleeper

I'm an Olympic sleeper—
      not one of those
      runners, skaters,
      skiers, boxers,
      wrestlers, or
heavy weight lifters.

Even lying supinely on the luge
      can seem too
      strenuous
      to those who
      doze soundly
around the clock
      with ease
      & who drift off
      promptly, too,
      if our cue
is somewhat musical
      (no starter pistol,
      please).

That there's no official event
      for fully trained
      slumberers—
      no teams,
      no judges,
      no TV coverage—
I most languidly lament.

Nonetheless, in my obscurity,
      I remain
      unique,
      unperturbed,
      & content.

Beyond all the bright lights,
      medals,
      or fame,
      in darkness
      & silence,
I still reign supreme
      in my own
      sweet calm
& my great Olympic dream.

Manatees

The state park at Blue Springs
        is like an aquarium,
        except you saunter
        out of doors
& the fish, manatees, & turtles
        float by below you
        in teal-blue
        Florida waters.

The giant so-called sea cattle
        appear so divinely
at peace—so loopy, bovine,
        & other worldly—
that you want to ignore
        the big posted sign
        & take a plunge
off the wooden walkway
        into the estuary,
        throwing your arms
around one of their chubby necks
        & swimming silently
        along with them
        down the little channel
till both you & the cows come home.

O Boy, O Boy!

Growing up in Oklahoma,
        nothing seemed
        so fun or crucial
        to me & my friends
        as football,
& most of us suffered
        the broken hopes
        & dismal fate
        of those who
        showed more grit
than talent or just dead weight.

We immortalized players
        & coaches
        we did not know
except by word of mouth,
        especially radio—
people with famous names
        like Bud Wilkinson,
        Jim Thorpe,
        Billy Vessels—
& of course, we disdained
        the Texas Longhorns
        & the Irish
        of Notre Dame.

I still follow quite faithfully
        any Oklahoma game,
        connecting via TV
        with feelings

of pride & shame of a sort
        because there's
something so provincial
        & primordial
        about this sport.

Nonetheless, this generation
        of mine
        won't finally
leave this game behind
        until we all
        cross over
some more ethereal
        goal line.

Stunner

It was the big, big win
        that wasn't any,
the perfect shot
        that really was not—
a great dramatic loss
        yanked
from the jaws of victory.

First came our brief
        celebration,
then the sudden
        devastation.

After much too much
        ballyhoo,
the referees grouped
        to officially state
what we all *now* believe:
        Buddy Hield's great
half-court heave
        left his right hand
just a little too late.[*]

---

[*] *This poem is about Oklahoma's 69-67 loss to West Virginia in the semifinal of the 2016 Big 12 Basketball Tournament.*

Her P-u-r-r

Is God responsible for all our pain?
           If not, how is it even possible,
unless She's somehow irresponsible
           & all we value useless or inane?

Enormous questions for the human brain,
           & some say, even more improbable
for kitten, dog, or other animal
           to ponder, weigh, reject, or ascertain.

By day, our tabby plays the splendid sphinx,
           reveals no cares except perhaps to stare,
or sleep & dream of worlds we're unaware;
           resolving ancient riddles, if she thinks.

But let us get to bed, and most nights her
           sole concern is petting & a grateful p-u-r-r.

SEATTLE SIGHT

One thing about living way out here
  in sometimes gloomy
  lumber land
  near a giant
  named Rainier,
is that—though it might
  seem at times
  to wander
  off somewhere
clear out of human sight—
  you sense the proud
  old mount
always being somewhere up there
  & beaming,
  noon or night,
with its majestic head,
  snow white,
high above the cloud banks,
  perpetually
  drenched
  by sun or moon
  in purest light.

Facelift for Garrison Hall

They've restored that dwelling
  across the way,
though it wasn't showing
  much decay.
It's taken months of dust, noise,
  & disarray,
not to mention the huge outlay.

Now, stick by stick, they deconstruct,
  hoping that dusk
  won't interrupt.
Those stacked catwalks are in the way
  of a fresh façade's
  light of day.

A man who never seems to stop
  has been lowering timbers
  from the top
of scaffolding still rifling the air,
  for possible reuse
  who knows where.

For me, it's been like theatre there.
  I'm one who likes
  to sit & stare,
contemplate how best to bear
  the ravages
  of time & wear.

Now that all their dirty work's done,
       here's for me the apparent sum:
Till life's somehow perfected here,
       more's to be done some other year.*

---

* *Garrison Hall is on Garrison Street in the South End of Boston.*

www.ingramcontent.com/pod-product-compliance
Lightning Source LLC
LaVergne TN
LVHW051701080426
835511LV00017B/2663